The Art

of

Recovery

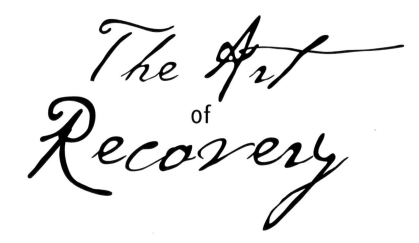

The Art of Recovery

A reflective and creative path
through the twelve steps

WHITNEY NOBIS

TATE PUBLISHING & Enterprises

Published by Tate Publishing & Enterprises, LLC
127 E. Trade Center Terrace | Mustang, Oklahoma 73064 USA
1.888.361.9473 | www.tatepublishing.com

Tate Publishing is committed to excellence in the publishing industry. The company reflects the philosophy established by the founders, based on Psalm 68:11,
"The Lord gave the word and great was the company of those who published it."

Book design copyright © 2009 by Tate Publishing, LLC. All rights reserved.
Cover design by Kandi Evans
Interior design by Lindsay B. Behrens

Published in the United States of America

ISBN: 978-1-61566-257-9
1. Self-help / Substance Abuse & Addictions / General
2. Self-help / Twelve-Step Programs
09.10.28

ACKNOWLEDGMENTS

There are many special people who have made this book a reality. First, my professors at Emporia State University, Gaelynn Wolf-Bordonaro and Libby Schmanke, played an instrumental part in guiding my ideas and shaping them into something tangible. My coworkers at Corner House Inc., Ashley Countryman and Sarah Riley-Hansen, taught me much about the field of substance abuse counseling. It was during this time I discovered how art therapy could play such a vital role in the recovery of addiction. My parents, Susan Pierson and Michael and Jacque O'Connor, as well as my in-laws, Mike and Pam Nobis, have given me nothing short of absolute support and guidance during this endeavor. Lastly, I owe much gratitude to my husband, Tom, for his steadfast love and unwavering dedication to me and my dreams. Thank you to you all!

TABLE OF CONTENTS

FOREWORD

I have been honored to witness the evolution of this book since its conception during the author's graduate art therapy internship at a substance abuse treatment center. Whitney's excitement about creating this helpful tool has been contagious, and I am delighted that her commitment to the project continued beyond graduation and now bears fruit.

The Art of Recovery provides a unique approach to working the twelve steps. No right or wrong answers are given; readers are encouraged to define important concepts for themselves. This approach is wise in addressing persons in early recovery who tend to resist anything that might be perceived as doctrinaire. At the same time, Whitney provides reassuring structure when appropriate, such as chart formats for the daunting work of steps four and eight. Her tone in the introduction is comforting and supportive. Informative and inspirational quotations and themes are given for each step.

Whitney's selection and development of art activities, from the tried-and-true "road drawing" to her own special spin on "artist trading cards," are thoughtfully matched to the twelve steps. Her format for the step work engages an ideal balance of concrete and metaphorical thinking processes. Written workbook questions are followed by nonverbal art activities. A final switch back to written reflection may uncover previously hidden meaning in the art and creates a deeper personal understanding of each step.

Although there are other addiction workbooks on the market, none has this one's built-in encouragement of the creative mind. With the simple addition of some colored pencils or markers, a glue stick, and a few old magazines for collage images, anyone can create a personal portfolio directly within these pages. The book will provide meaning not only as it is worked but as a keepsake and conduit to deeper understanding in future years.

The Art of Recovery is the workbook I will turn to for any of my private practice clients with addiction issues. I believe it will be a useful tool not only for those first learning about the twelve steps but also for anyone working a lifelong program of recovery. So, Whitney, congratulations and thanks! I know I won't be the only one who is grateful for your gift.

—Libby Schmanke, MS, ATR-BC
Board-Certified Art Therapist
State-Certified Substance Abuse Counselor
Faculty, Emporia State University

INTRODUCTION

Recovery from an addiction can be scary, intimidating, and a lot of work. To help you through the process, *The Art of Recovery* has been developed, offering you a safe outlet to express your feelings, discover new coping skills, and learn new ways to think about things. *The Art of Recovery* is a twelve-step workbook that will carefully lead you through inward reflection and outward action by asking thoughtful questions and using therapeutic (and fun) art directives.

The Art of Recovery utilizes the benefits of art therapy, a treatment method that offers unlimited possibilities for growth, renewal, and strength. Art making can help you face life's problems, connect with others, and gain a deeper relationship with yourself. It can help you uncover nonverbal cues that are sometimes locked away in your unconscious. New discoveries, creative outcomes, heightened awareness, and deep understanding are but a few of the rewards you will find through the making of art. And the best part is you do not have to be artistic to use this workbook!

Remember to work through this time of your life at your own pace. Embrace and enjoy the process of *The Art of Recovery!*

SUGGESTED MATERIALS

The materials suggested for the art making are merely suggestions. You are free to use what you feel comfortable with and what you are able to acquire. There are no limits!

Art Journal

- This can be a drawing pad, a notebook with blank pages, or simply white paper kept together in a binder.
- It is advised that the paper be at least eight and a half inches by eleven inches so there is plenty of room for your creative expression.

Index Cards

Drawing Materials

- Pencils
- Colored Pencils

- Markers

- Crayons

- Paints

- Oil/Chalk Pastels

Collage Materials

- Magazines, newspapers, fabrics, cards, etc.

- Scissors

- Glue sticks

Use materials with which you feel most comfortable. There is no right or wrong way to complete the directives. Simply have fun and enjoy the process!

HOW IT WORKS

Each step in the workbook follows the same layout. The first section contains reflective questions pertaining to the step at hand. Next, you will be introduced to several art activities. Read through the whole directive first and then complete the activity in your art journal. To complete the process, there is a space for written reflection concerning each piece of artwork. Take time to look over what you created and write your thoughts, feelings, and insights.

This workbook is not intended to be the sole tool in your recovery process. There are other important factors that may also play a role in your journey, such as a treatment facility, therapist/counselor, sponsor, family, and friends. It is encouraged to use this workbook in conjunction with one or more of these sources, especially if you are faced with confusion or frustration. Do not feel as though you are in this alone!

It is important to keep this workbook in a safe, secure place. Your work is your own. You need to feel as though you are able to be rigorously honest in your recovery journey. You would not want your inner recovery process falling into the hands of someone who would jeopardize your progress. Therefore, find a safe location to keep both this workbook and your art journal.

Recovery from an addiction may be the hardest work you ever do. Work through this important time of your life at your own pace. *Be patient with your progress and enjoy the journey!*

TWELVE STEPS IN THE ART OF RECOVERY

Step One: We admitted we were powerless over substance dependence, that our lives had become unmanageable.

Step Two: We came to believe that a power greater than ourselves could restore us to sanity.

Step Three: We made a decision to turn our will and our lives over to the care of our Higher Power.

Step Four: We made a searching and fearless moral inventory of ourselves.

Step Five: We admitted to our Higher Power, to ourselves, and to another human being the exact nature of our wrongs.

Step Six: We were entirely ready to have our Higher Power remove all these defects of character.

Step Seven: We humbly asked him to remove our shortcomings.

Step Eight: We made a list of all persons we had harmed and became willing to make amends to them all.

Step Nine: We made direct amends to such people wherever possible, except when to do so would injure them or others.

Step Ten: We continued to take a personal inventory and when we were wrong promptly admitted it.

Step Eleven: We sought through prayer and meditation to improve our conscious contact with our Higher Power, praying only for knowledge of his will for us and the power to carry that out.

Step Twelve: Having had a spiritual awakening as a result of these steps, we tried to carry this message to others and to practice these principles in all our affairs.

STEP ONE

We admitted we were powerless over substance dependence, that our lives had become unmanageable.

If you are reading this, then at some point you have become aware of an issue in your life you wish to work on or change. A lot of times we are aware of problems in our lives, yet we have a hard time accepting them. Acceptance can be scary, because with acceptance comes responsibility, the responsibility of becoming accountable for our feelings and behaviors. It can be a daunting process to see how different areas of your life have become unmanageable. However, with acceptance also comes freedom! You now have the chance to honestly look at your life and begin picking up the pieces you have for so long overlooked. The following questions allow you the opportunity to examine and focus on your level of acceptance and recognize certain areas of powerlessness in your life.

Questions

Define the following terms in your own words:

We admitted

_____

_____

We were powerless

_____

_____

Our lives had become unmanageable

_____

_____

What does this step mean to you?

_____

_____

_____

Write this step in your own words.

_____

_____

_____

_____

_____

_____

ART DIRECTIVE

1.1 Life Line

Goals:
- To create a map of your life.
- To recognize both the positive and the negative events that occurred in your life.
- To compare the positive life events with the negative life events and see if this correlates with your substance use history.
- To recognize turning points in your substance use history.

Materials:
- Paper (larger paper preferred)
- Drawing supplies (markers, colored pencils, pencils, pens, etc.)

Directions:
Draw a line across the middle of the paper. Place positive life events above the line and negative life events below the line. If you wish, you can choose a specific color for the positive and another for the negative. Also, images are a great addition to depict your memories of past events. Start back as far as you feel comfortable (from birth is great!) and end with today. You can include events such as starting school, graduations, job losses, first drug use, incarcerations, relationships, etc. Feel free to use additional paper if needed.

Example:

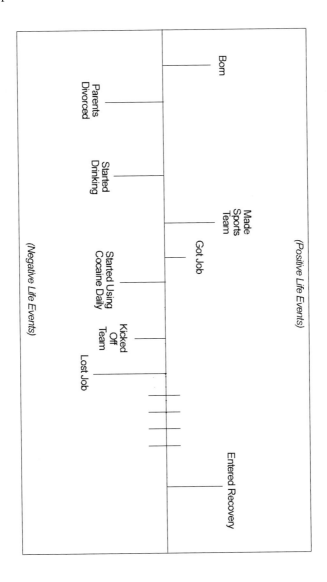

(Positive Life Events)

Born

Made Sports Team

Got Job

Entered Recovery

Parents Divorced

Started Drinking

Started Using Cocaine Daily

Kicked Off Team

Lost Job

(Negative Life Events)

LIFE LINE: WRITTEN REFLECTIONS

What was this experience like for you?

_____

_____

What is the most interesting part of your life line?

_____

_____

_____

Did you use any specific colors? Explain.

_____

_____

_____

How do you feel when you look at your life line?

_____

_____

_____

_____

Did you find any correlations between positive events and substance use? Negative events and substance use?

_____

_____

_____

_____

_____

_____

_____

What did you learn about yourself by doing this activity?

_____

_____

_____

_____

ACCEPTANCE

What does acceptance mean to you?

_____

_____

_____

What is the hardest part of acceptance for you?

_____

_____

_____

_____

Have you been able to accept things in the past that have been difficult for you?

_____

_____

_____

How did you do this?

_____

_____

_____

_____

ART DIRECTIVE

1.2 Picture of Powerlessness

Goals:
- To reflect on the feelings evoked through being powerless.
- To identify what your personal powerlessness looks like.
- To create an awareness of times in which you are powerless.

Materials:
- Paper
- Drawing supplies (markers, colored pencils, pencils, pens, etc.)

Directions:
Draw a picture representing your personal powerlessness.

Keep in mind the following questions: How do you feel when you are powerless? How do you behave when you are powerless? What thoughts do you have when you are powerless? What does it look like when you are powerless?

PICTURE OF POWERLESSNESS: WRITTEN REFLECTIONS

What was this experience like for you?

_____

_____

_____

What images emerged in your drawing?

_____

_____

_____

_____

Were you surprised by the finished drawing?

_____

_____

_____

In what situations are you most often powerless?

_____

_____

_____

_____

How does it feel to visually depict your powerlessness?

_____

_____

_____

_____

What did you learn about yourself by doing this activity?

_____

_____

_____

POWERLESSNESS

What does powerlessness mean to you?

_____

_____

_____

List ways you have become powerless over your addiction.

_____

_____

_____

_____

How do you know when you are powerless?

_____

_____

_____

_____

What does powerlessness feel like?

_____

_____

_____

_____

Art Directive

1.3 Collage of Chaos

Goals:

- To identify areas of your life that have become chaotic.
- To express your feelings toward past events of powerlessness.
- To clarify what situations brought about the most chaos.

Materials:

- Paper (larger paper preferred)
- Collage materials, scissors, glue
- Drawing supplies (markers, colored pencils, pencils, pens, etc.)

Directions:

Make a collage illustrating the chaos produced in your life as a result of your addiction. Use the scissors to cut out the images you want to use and glue them to the paper. Think about past arguments, disappointments, pain, heartache, etc.

(If collage materials are not available to you, sketch out related images using drawing supplies.)

COLLAGE OF CHAOS: WRITTEN REFLECTIONS

What was this experience like for you?

_____

_____

_____

What would you title this collage?

_____

_____

What did you include in the collage to depict the chaos? Why?

_____

_____

_____

_____

What does it feel like to look at your collage of chaos?

_____

_____

_____

_____

What did you learn about yourself by doing this activity?

_____

_____

_____

_____

_____

UNMANAGEABILITY

What does it mean to you to be unmanageable?

_____

_____

_____

How has your life become unmanageable?

_____

_____

_____

What area of your life is the most unmanageable? What feeling would you associate with this?

_____

_____

_____

_____

_____

_____

How do you feel when your life is unmanageable?

_____

_____

Do you receive feedback from friends or family about your substance use? If so, what kind of feedback?

_____

_____

_____

_____

_____

What changes are you willing to make to admit powerlessness and unmanageability?

_____

_____

_____

_____

What have you done so far? What do you still need to complete?

_____

_____

_____

_____

How is this step essential to your recovery?

_____

_____

_____

_____

"I admit I am powerless over _____ , that my life has become unmanageable."

And acceptance is the answer to *all* my problems today. When I am disturbed, it is because I find some person, place, thing, or situation—some fact of my life—unacceptable to me, and I can find no serenity until I accept that person, place, thing, or situation as being exactly the way it is supposed to be at this moment. Nothing, absolutely nothing, happens in God's world by mistake. Until I could accept my alcoholism, I could not stay sober; unless I accept life completely on life's terms, I cannot be happy. I need to concentrate not so much on what needs to be changed in the world as on what needs to be changed in me and in my attitudes.

Alcoholics Anonymous, 2001, p. 417

Before moving on to the next step, take a moment to review what you have accomplished thus far. It is critical you have an acceptance of the problem you are working on, as acceptance is the starting point of all change. Ask yourself: Do I have a general understanding and acceptance of my substance dependence? Have I identified areas of my life that are unmanageable, as well as examined my level of powerlessness over my use of substances?

If you feel comfortable sharing this experience with a therapist, friend, or family member, take the time to talk to them about how this experience was for you and about any insights or realizations you have come across during this step.

STEP TWO

We came to believe that a power greater than ourselves could restore us to sanity.

> Again I say, all you need is the open mind.
>
> *Twelve Steps and Twelve Traditions,* 1981, p. 26

QUESTIONS

Define the following terms in your own words:

Came to believe

_____

_____

Power greater than ourselves

_____

_____

Restore

_____

_____

Sanity

_____

_____

What does this step mean to you?

_____

_____

Write this step in your own words.

_____

_____

BELIEVE

We all have certain beliefs that shape who we are and how we act. Our set of beliefs and attitudes typically come from how we were raised. Examples include beliefs on religion, spirituality, culture, heritage, work ethic, and family relations. The following questions ask you to reflect on and identify your thoughts and feelings about believing in something.

What does it mean to believe in something?

_____

_____

_____

_____

_____

How does it feel to believe in something?

_____

_____

_____

_____

What are some things you personally believe in?

_____

_____

_____

_____

_____

ART DIRECTIVE

2.1 Image of Higher Power

Goals:
- To express how something bigger than yourself may help with your recovery process.
- To identify how your Higher Power relates to your recovery.
- To develop a tangible image or symbol of your Higher Power.

Materials:
- Paper
- Drawing supplies (markers, colored pencils, pencils, pens, etc.)

Directions:

Draw your Higher Power. There is no right or wrong answer for this activity. Keep in mind the following questions: What does your Higher Power look like? Think? Do? Feel? How does your Higher Power act? Help you? Help others?

IMAGE OF HIGHER POWER: WRITTEN REFLECTIONS

What was this experience like for you?

_____

_____

_____

_____

Describe your drawing. How did you depict your Higher Power?

_____

_____

_____

_____

How does it feel to have an image of your Higher Power?

_____

_____

_____

_____

If you're ambivalent about having a Higher Power, did this activity help you conceptualize one? If so, explain.

_____

_____

_____

_____

_____

What title would you give your Higher Power?

_____

What did you learn about yourself by doing this activity?

_____

_____

_____

_____

HIGHER POWER

The main theme for Step Two is *faith*. Faith is like taking a leap into the unknown and trusting in something that is not always visible. This can seem scary, even impossible for some people. Yet for others it is a highly welcomed idea. Think of the possibility of not *having* to be in control of *everything*. What a concept! Having a Higher Power in your recovery process is very important. For some, the idea of a Higher Power is God. For others, it may be a support group or family unit. Either way, now is the time to think about your Higher Power and start believing in its role in your recovery.

Define *Higher Power* in your own terms.

_____

_____

_____

_____

What do you believe constitutes a Higher Power?

_____

_____

_____

_____

Describe your thoughts and beliefs about a Higher Power.

_____

_____

_____

_____

_____

_____

Do you have a Higher Power? If so, explain.

_____

_____

_____

_____

_____

How can your Higher Power help you through your addiction?

_____

_____

_____

_____

_____

Why do you believe it is important to have a Higher Power in recovery?

_____

_____

_____

_____

How would it feel to have a Higher Power helping you in recovery?

_____

_____

_____

_____

RESTORE TO SANITY

The classic definition of insanity is doing the same thing over and over and expecting different results. Addiction has a way of bringing about insanity in everyone it touches in some way or another. Therefore, it is in the recovery process where you seek to regain the sanity you once had. It is time to restore your mind and body back to its pre-addiction state.

What does *restore* mean to you?

_____

_____

_____

_____

What would you like to be restored to?

_____

_____

_____

Define what *sanity* means to you.

_____

_____

_____

_____

Do you feel you have ever experienced a time of sanity? What was
going right in your life during this time?

_____

_____

_____

_____

_____

_____

_____

Define what *insanity* means to you.

_____

_____

_____

_____

_____

_____

Do you feel you have ever experienced a time of insanity? What was going wrong in your life during this time?

_____

_____

_____

_____

_____

_____

_____

On a scale of one to ten, ten being the highest, how confident are you that a power greater than yourself could restore you to sanity? Explain.

_____

_____

_____

_____

_____

_____

If below ten, what would need to take place to move you closer to ten? Explain.

_____

_____

_____

_____

_____

Are you ready and willing to try to let a power greater than yourself restore you to sanity? If yes, explain how you are ready and willing. If no, how will you know when you are ready and willing?

_____

_____

_____

_____

_____

Preparing for Step Three, how will you ask to be "restored to sanity"?

_____

_____

_____

_____

_____

_____

Have you ever experienced a time when a power greater than yourself did something for you that you could not do for yourself? Explain.

_____

_____

_____

_____

_____

How is this step essential to your recovery?

_____

_____

_____

_____

_____

ART DIRECTIVE

2.2 Bridge to Recovery

Goals:

- To encourage you to think about the past and what your future may hold.

- To recognize possible roadblocks in your recovery.

- To identify which direction you are heading in your recovery.

Materials:

- Paper

- Drawing supplies (markers, colored pencils, pencils, pens, etc.)

Directions:

Draw a bridge that connects your addiction to your recovery. Place yourself someplace in the drawing and with an arrow indicate which direction you are moving. Think of the following questions: What kind of bridge is it? Are there supports? Are they visible? How is your bridge put together? What surrounds your bridge? Is your bridge long or short?

BRIDGE TO RECOVERY: WRITTEN REFLECTIONS

What was this experience like for you?

_____

_____

_____

_____

_____

Describe your bridge.

_____

_____

_____

_____

_____

Why did you place yourself where you did on your bridge?

_____

_____

_____

_____

What supports, if any, do you see in your bridge?

_____

_____

_____

How might these supports, or lack of supports, be a metaphor for your recovery?

_____

_____

_____

_____

What does it feel like to look at your bridge?

_____

_____

_____

_____

What did you learn about yourself by doing this activity?

_____

_____

_____

_____

_____

Review the work you have completed in Step Two. Have you hon-estly accepted the idea of a Higher Power working in your life, and do you honestly accept the fact that your Higher Power can restore you to sanity? If you still have doubts with this step, it is recommended you talk with a therapist, sponsor, friend, or family member for support and additional insight. Please make sure you feel comfortable with this step before moving forward.

STEP THREE

We made a decision to turn our will and our lives over to the care of our Higher Power.

QUESTIONS

Define the following terms in your own words:

Made a decision

_____

_____

Will

_____

_____

Life

_____

_____

Care of our Higher Power

_____

_____

What does this step mean to you?

_____

_____

_____

Write this step in your own words.

_____

_____

_____

_____

Have you ever surrendered to anything before? Explain.

_____

_____

_____

_____

_____

What thoughts come to mind when you hear the word *surrender?* What feelings?

_____

_____

_____

_____

_____

_____

_____

_____

The more we become willing to depend upon a higher power, the more independent we actually are.

Twelve Steps and Twelve Traditions, 1981, p. 36

Art Directive

3.1 My Will

Goals:
- To explore reasons as to why self-will is important to you.
- To identify roadblocks self-will creates in your recovery.
- To promote a desire to reevaluate your self-will.

Materials:
- Paper
- Drawing supplies (markers, colored pencils, pencils, pens, etc.)

Directions:
Create an image of your self-will. What does your self-will look like? Is it stubborn? Willful? Obstinate? Controlling? Unreasonable? Manipulative?

MY WILL: WRITTEN REFLECTIONS

What was this experience like for you?

_____

_____

_____

What emerged from your image?

_____

_____

_____

Are you surprised by what you created? Explain.

_____

_____

_____

_____

How do you see your self-will interfering with your recovery?

_____

_____

_____

How would you title your drawing?

_____

_____

What did you learn about yourself by doing this activity?

_____

_____

_____

_____

YOUR WILL

Your will or determination is what motivates you to do the things
you do. Is your will strong and aggressive, or weak and passive? The
following questions ask you to think about your personal will and
ways in which it has affected your life.

How would you describe *your* will?

_____

_____

_____

_____

How important is your will?

_____

_____

_____

_____

In what ways has your will hurt you in the past?

_____

_____

_____

_____

How has it helped you?

_____

_____

_____

_____

What does it mean to turn your will over to a power greater than yourself?

_____

_____

_____

_____

_____

ART DIRECTIVE

3.2 Turning-It-Over Collage

Goals:

- To problem-solve different ways of letting go of your self-will.
- To gain an understanding of how letting go of self-will can aid in your recovery.
- To imagine life connected with your Higher Power.

Materials:

- Paper (larger paper preferred)
- Collage materials, scissors, glue
- Drawing supplies (markers, colored pencils, pencils, pens, etc.)

Directions:
Make a collage illustrating what it will look like when you turn over your life to a Higher Power.

(If collage materials are not available to you, sketch out related images using drawing materials.)

TURNING-IT-OVER COLLAGE: WRITTEN REFLECTIONS

What was this experience like for you?

_____

_____

_____

What items did you place in the collage? How are you turning your will over to your Higher Power?

_____

_____

_____

_____

_____

How does it feel to look at this collage?

_____

_____

_____

_____

What would you title this collage?

_____

_____

What did you learn about yourself by doing this activity?

_____

_____

_____

_____

_____

YOUR LIFE

No one knows your life better than yourself. Take a moment and think about your life as a whole. What does your life mean to you? To others? How have you been handling your life? Once you have decided there is a power greater than yourself that can restore you to sanity, you need to make a decision. Will you turn your will and your life over? Surrendering to a Higher Power does not take personal responsibility away from you or your actions. Rather, it assists you in reducing any worry you may carry and offers you continual, daily support.

Describe your life using only three words. Is this how you would like your life to look?

_____

_____

_____

_____

How does it feel when someone else tells you what to do? How do you behave when others tell you what to do?

_____

_____

_____

_____

What does it mean to turn your life over?

_____

_____

_____

_____

How do you turn your life over to something you may not be able to see?

_____

_____

_____

_____

_____

What reservations do you have in taking this step? Explain.

_____

_____

_____

_____

_____

How will these be overcome?

_____

_____

_____

_____

_____

What will you struggle most with in regards to this step?

_____

_____

_____

_____

How can these things be overcome or dealt with?

_____

_____

_____

_____

Create your own personal prayer or admission of surrendering.

_____

_____

_____

_____

_____

What will it look like or how will others know if you have taken this step?

_____

_____

_____

_____

What benefits do you think you will receive as a result of taking this step?

_____

_____

_____

_____

What do you want most from your Higher Power?

_____

_____

_____

_____

What do you think your Higher Power has in store for you?

_____

_____

_____

_____

How is this step essential to your recovery?

_____

_____

_____

_____

ART DIRECTIVE

3.3 Circles of Strength

Goals:
- To identify positive characteristics about yourself.
- To receive positive feedback from other people important in your life.
- To gain a feeling of self-worth and validation by focusing on your strengths.

Materials:
- Paper
- Drawing supplies (markers, colored pencils, pencils, pens, etc.)

Directions:

In the center of your paper, trace three circles, one inside of the other, as shown in the example on the following page. Fill in the center circle with your name and decorate the circle to show your personality. The middle circle should be filled in with words that describe you. Fill in the third circle with specific roles that you serve (such as son, daughter, student, etc.). Lastly, on the page outside the circles, ask important people in your life (family, friends, sponsor, fellowship from support meetings) to write one positive comment about you.

Example:

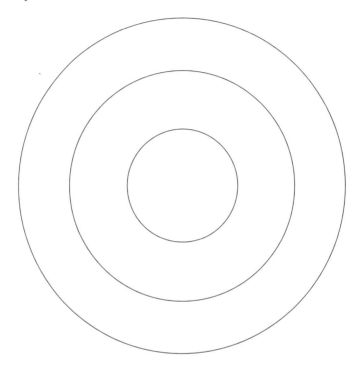

CIRCLES OF STRENGTH: WRITTEN REFLECTIONS

What was this experience like for you?

_____

_____

_____

What was the hardest part of this activity?

_____

_____

_____

_____

How did it feel to write positive things about yourself?

_____

_____

_____

_____

How did it feel to read positive things that other people wrote about you?

_____

_____

_____

Do you agree with the statements from other people? Explain.

_____

_____

_____

What did you learn about yourself by doing this activity?

_____

_____

_____

_____

_____

_____

_____

_____

By now, it is my hope you have come to some sort of peace with your decision to quit using substances. Go back to the prayer or admission of surrender you created earlier in this chapter. I recommend you recite this statement every morning, or at least as often as you can. An important part of the recovery process is living every day just for that day. Every morning offers us a new beginning and a fresh opportunity. Be sure to utilize every chance you have for growth.

STEP FOUR

We made a searching and fearless moral inventory of ourselves.

Resentment is the number-one offender.

Alcoholics Anonymous, 2001, p. 64

QUESTIONS

Define the following terms in your own words:

Searching

_____

_____

Fearless

_____

_____

Moral

_____

_____

Inventory

_____

_____

What does this step mean to you?

_____

_____

_____

_____

Write this step in your own words.

_____

_____

_____

ART DIRECTIVE

4.1 Wall Drawing

Goals:

- To identify and understand your personal defenses.
- To reflect on feelings and situations in which your defenses go up.
- To gain an awareness of how your personal defenses may affect other people.

Materials:

- Paper
- Drawing supplies (markers, colored pencils, pencils, pens, etc.)

Directions:

Think about how you protect yourself emotionally. How do you keep people out or away? How do you keep yourself in? If you could build a wall around yourself, what would it look like? Now, draw this image.

WALL DRAWING: WRITTEN REFLECTIONS

What was this experience like for you?

_____

_____

_____

What does your wall look like? Describe it.

_____

_____

_____

_____

Do you feel this is an accurate depiction of how you keep others out? Explain.

_____

_____

_____

_____

_____

How does it feel to look at your wall?

_____

_____

_____

How do you think others perceive this wall?

_____

_____

_____

What did you learn about yourself by doing this activity?

_____

_____

_____

_____

_____

After completing the first three steps, it is time to start taking an honest look at your past behaviors, fears, resentments, relationships, and responsibilities. Step Four can be hard for many to work through, as it requires a careful and thorough look back on items that may be painful. There may be items from your past you do not want to think about or remember. However, it is critical you write out everything and be honest with yourself.

It is common to experience an increase in sad feelings and/or an increase in the urge to return to the addicted behavior. Therefore, it is a good idea to have a plan of action should you experience such things. Know what happened in the past is in the past. Understand that by revisiting or recalling past actions and feelings does not mean you have to return to them. This is simply a chance to come to terms with and examine your past actions, as well as how your use of substances played a role in them.

What do you believe a moral inventory should contain?

_____

_____

_____

_____

_____

Have you ever taken a moral inventory of yourself? If so, explain.

_____

_____

_____

What reservations do you have about taking this step?

_____

_____

_____

Where do you think those reservations come from? How can they be overcome?

_____

_____

_____

_____

_____

_____

How is honesty critical in taking this step?

_____

_____

_____

_____

The following charts were created to assist you in writing out your moral inventory. There is an example at the beginning of each chart to help guide you through each section. Please do not feel intimidated by this exercise. Take your time and work at a comfortable pace. If you feel you need more room to write things out, use your art journal for additional space.

RESENTMENTS

Having resentment toward someone or something only hurts you. Most often, the other person does not even know you are feeling that way. In recovery, there is little room for ill will or hateful feelings toward others. Focusing on and finding ways to better yourself is what recovery is all about. The following section allows you the opportunity to list the people toward whom you feel resentment. In the spaces provided, list every reason you resent that person, how this feeling of resentment affects you personally, and the character defects you suffer as a result of these resentments.

Example:

Person: Father

RESENTMENT	AFFECTS my...	Resulting Character Defects
Worked too much	Self-esteem, security, personal relationship	Anger, envy, pride, jealousy

Your Resentments:

Person: _____

RESENTMENT	AFFECTS my...	Resulting Character Defects

Person: _____

RESENTMENT	AFFECTS my…	Resulting Character Defects

Person: _____

RESENTMENT	AFFECTS my…	Resulting Character Defects

Person: _____

RESENTMENT	AFFECTS my…	Resulting Character Defects

Person: _____

RESENTMENT	AFFECTS my...	Resulting Character Defects

FEARS

In the spaces provided, list the fears you have in your life, why you fear these things, and how you feel as a result.

Example:

FEAR	Why You Fear This	Resulting Feelings from the Fear
Abandonment	Because I can't live my life by myself	Worthlessness, self-pity, anger

Your Fears:

FEAR	Why You Fear This	Resulting Feelings from the Fear

RELATIONSHIPS

In the spaces provided, list the people that have been directly affected by your alcohol or drug use. Then explain how they have been affected and your resulting feelings.

Example:

Relationship	Affected by...	Resulting Feelings
Best Friend	My lying and stealing	Untrustworthy, sad, disappointed

Your Relationships:

Relationship	Affected by...	Resulting Feelings

RESPONSIBILITIES

In the spaces provided, list the responsibilities you have avoided during your use, who you may blame for your actions, and your resulting feelings.

Example:

I Lack Responsibility For	I Blame	Resulting Feelings
Picking up kids after practice	Wife/husband for not reminding me	Anger, disappointment

Your Responsibilities:

I Lack Responsibility For	I Blame	Resulting Feelings

How is this step essential to your recovery?

_____

_____

_____

_____

How do you feel after thoroughly and completely finishing this step?

_____

_____

_____

_____

ART DIRECTIVE

4.2 Ugly Picture Drawing

Goals:
- To begin to appreciate every aspect of your personality and character.
- To realize every person has some unique qualities of beauty in him or her.
- To recognize and move past your imperfections and flaws.

Materials:
- Paper
- Drawing supplies (markers, colored pencils, pencils, pens, etc.)

Directions:
Draw the ugliest picture you can of whatever you want. When you're done, tear it out and put a frame around it, if you like. Hang this picture up and live with it for a while. Do you notice any change in your feelings about it?

UGLY PICTURE DRAWING: WRITTEN REFLECTIONS

What was this experience like for you?

_____

_____

_____

How did you make this picture as ugly as you could?

_____

_____

_____

What makes it ugly?

_____

_____

_____

Was it still ugly after you hung it up with a frame and looked at it for a while? Explain.

_____

_____

_____

_____

_____

What would you title this drawing? Explain.

_____

_____

_____

_____

What did you learn about yourself by doing this activity?

_____

_____

_____

_____

ART DIRECTIVE

4.3 Secret Drawing

Goals:
- To express or represent a secret in a drawing.
- To reflect on secrets you are keeping from others and perhaps from yourself.
- To release something into an image that has been causing you pain or heartache.

Materials:
- Paper
- Drawing supplies (markers, colored pencils, pencils, pens, etc.)

Directions:
Draw a secret that has been bothering you lately. You may use symbols if you do not wish to depict the exact image.

SECRET DRAWING: WRITTEN REFLECTIONS

What was this experience like for you?

_____

_____

_____

How did it feel to express your secret in a drawing?

_____

_____

_____

_____

Describe how you depicted your secret.

_____

_____

_____

_____

Are you ready to share this secret with anyone? If so, who?

_____

_____

What did you learn about yourself by doing this activity?

_____

_____

_____

_____

_____

Focusing on yourself is not always a fun thing to do. Look back over the previous charts. Do you think you left any information out? As previously stated, use your art journal for additional writing room if you need to add more information. This is hard work! But you are doing it and you are worth it!

Do one thing for *you* today. You deserve it!

STEP FIVE

We admitted to our Higher Power, to ourselves, and to another human being the exact nature of our wrongs.

> We must be entirely honest with somebody if we expect to live long or happily in this world.
>
> *Alcoholics Anonymous,* 2001, p. 74

QUESTIONS

Define the following terms in your own words:

Admitted

_____

_____

Exact Nature

_____

_____

Wrongs

_____

_____

What does this step mean to you?

_____

_____

_____

_____

Write this step in your own words.

_____

_____

_____

ART DIRECTIVE

5.1 Broken Wall Drawing

Goals:

- To increase personal strength in your abilities to interact with yourself and other people without the use of extreme defenses.

- To explore what it would be like if you lessened your defenses in recovery.

- To brainstorm different ways of letting go of your defenses.

Materials:

- Paper

- Drawing supplies (markers, colored pencils, pencils, pens, etc.)

Directions:

Think back to the wall drawing you did in Step Four. Imagine what it would be like if you did not have the constraints of that wall surrounding you from your life. Draw the wall again, but this time broken down.

BROKEN WALL DRAWING: WRITTEN REFLECTIONS

What was this experience like for you?

_____

_____

_____

What does your broken wall look like?

_____

_____

_____

_____

Compare this drawing to the previous one in Step Four. What similarities and differences do you see in them?

_____

_____

_____

_____

_____

_____

How does it feel to look at your broken wall?

_____

_____

_____

_____

What did you learn about yourself by doing this activity?

_____

_____

_____

_____

Telling another person your darkest secrets and past behaviors is not something that comes easily to most people. The following questions give you the opportunity to explore your thoughts and/or fears in sharing with someone what you wrote in Step Four.

How do you feel about sharing your Step Four with your Higher Power, yourself, and another person?

_____

_____

_____

_____

What reservations do you have with this step?

_____

_____

_____

_____

What character traits are needed to take this step? Do you feel you have these character traits?

_____

_____

_____

_____

How does trust play a role in this step for you?

_____

_____

_____

_____

_____

Who will you be sharing this step with, and why did you choose that person?

_____

_____

_____

_____

_____

Do you feel you are able to trust this person with your moral inventory?

_____

_____

What do you think you will gain as a result of completing this step?

_____

_____

_____

_____

ART DIRECTIVE

5.2 Anger/Peace Collage

Goals:
- To visualize what your personal anger and peace look like.
- To identify feelings and behaviors associated with anger and peace.
- To compare your feelings of anger and peace visually and which one you feel your recovery falls under.

Materials:
- Paper (larger paper preferred)
- Collage materials, scissors, glue
- Drawing supplies (markers, colored pencils, pencils, pens, etc.)

Directions:
Using the collage materials, cut out images you feel represent both anger and peace. Glue them on the paper so that anger is on one side and peace is on the other side.

(If collage materials are not available to you, sketch out related images using drawing supplies.)

ANGER/PEACE COLLAGE: WRITTEN REFLECTIONS

What was this experience like for you?

_____

_____

_____

What images did you choose to represent anger? Peace?

_____

_____

_____

_____

What side do you feel your recovery falls under? Are you happy with this? If not, how can you make it different?

_____

_____

_____

_____

What side would you like your life to be on? How can you make that happen?

_____

_____

_____

_____

_____

What did you learn about yourself by doing this activity?

_____

_____

_____

_____

_____

Now is the time to complete this step with someone. Remember to choose someone with whom you feel safe and secure. Try to allow for at least one hour, preferably more, to complete this step. Avoid busy places to meet. Quiet areas such as someone's home, a church, or a quiet park are ideal locations. Be honest, open, and humble while sharing your story.

AFTER COMPLETING THIS STEP

How did sharing your past history make you feel? Explain.

_____

_____

_____

_____

_____

What was the hardest part of sharing your inventory?

_____

_____

_____

What do you feel you gained by completing this step?

_____

_____

_____

_____

How is this step essential to your recovery?

_____

_____

_____

_____

STEP SIX

We were entirely ready to have our Higher Power remove all these defects of character.

QUESTIONS

Define the following in your own words:

Entirely ready

_____

_____

Remove

_____

_____

Defects

_____

_____

Character

_____

_____

What does this step mean to you?

_____

_____

_____

_____

Write this step in your own words.

_____

_____

_____

Now that you have identified, examined, and shared past behaviors, relationships, attitudes, etc., it is time to make a personal change. No change can happen unless you *honestly* want it to happen. Have the previous five steps provided you with enough reason and motivation to *want* to change? I hope so!

Step Six will have you examine items you are willing and ready to have your Higher Power remove from your life. Review your resulting character defects and resulting feelings from your Step Four inventory. Are these things you want to continue to live with? Or be free from?

Hopefully Steps Four and Five have provided motivation for change. Which painful memories inspired you most to change?

_____

_____

_____

_____

_____

_____

How are you getting ready to make a change in your life?

_____

_____

_____

_____

_____

What changes are you planning to make?

_____

_____

_____

_____

What changes have you already made?

_____

_____

_____

_____

_____

Are you aware of the items you want your Higher Power to remove from your life?

_____

_____

ART DIRECTIVE

6.1 Picture of Personal Shortcomings

Goals:
- To identify various shortcomings you see in your life keeping you from moving forward in your recovery.
- To realize that you are not perfect, and do not have to be, in your recovery.
- To create a visual image connected to how you feel inside.

Materials:
- Paper
- Drawing supplies (markers, colored pencils, pencils, pens, etc.)

Directions:
Think back to the character defect you identified in Step Four. On your paper, create personal images that represent these defects of character.

PICTURE OF PERSONAL SHORTCOMINGS: WRITTEN REFLECTIONS

What was this experience like for you?

_____

_____

_____

What defects of character did you represent?

_____

_____

_____

How did you represent these in images?

_____

_____

_____

_____

How does it feel to look at the images you created?

_____

_____

_____

_____

What did you learn about yourself by doing this activity?

_____

_____

_____

_____

Please list the defects of character you are willing to have your Higher Power remove.

_____

_____

_____

_____

_____

How do you feel your life will be different if these defects of character are removed?

_____

_____

_____

_____

Do you feel *entirely ready* for your Higher Power to remove them?

_____

_____

If yes, explain how you have prepared yourself. If no, how will you become *entirely ready?*

_____

_____

_____

_____

How is this step essential to your recovery?

_____

_____

_____

_____

Art Directive

6.2 Five Years From Now Drawing

Goals:

- To begin thinking about where you see yourself in the near future.

- To explore a variety of possibilities and goals for your future.

- To learn what could be done today for these goals to become a reality.

Materials:

- Paper

- Drawing supplies (markers, colored pencils, pencils, pens, etc.)

Directions:

Draw where you see yourself in five years. Where will you be? What will you look like? What will you be doing? How will your relationships with others be?

FIVE YEARS FROM NOW DRAWING: WRITTEN REFLECTIONS

What was this experience like for you?

_____

_____

_____

Describe your drawing.

_____

_____

_____

_____

_____

_____

Are these realistic goals for you? Explain.

_____

_____

_____

_____

_____

What steps are you taking today to become closer to achieving your goals?

_____

_____

_____

_____

How would you title this drawing?

_____

_____

What did you learn about yourself by doing this activity?

_____

_____

_____

_____

_____

Identifying personal character defects may have been hard; however, you have to identify them in order to be free from them. It may be a good idea to consult with someone (perhaps the person you shared your moral inventory with) over what you selected for this section. He or she may have additional insight to share with you.

STEP SEVEN

We humbly asked him to remove our shortcomings.

> We ask especially for freedom from self-will, and are careful to make no request for ourselves only.
>
> *Alcoholics Anonymous,* 2001, p. 87

QUESTIONS

Define the following terms in your own words:

Humbly

_____

_____

Asked

_____

_____

Remove

_____

_____

Shortcomings

_____

_____

What does this step mean to you?

_____

_____

_____

_____

Write this step in your own words.

_____

_____

_____

HUMILITY

Humility is the state of being free from pride and arrogance. Humility may be hard for people in recovery, as addiction can be full of self-importance and overconfidence. Being humble is more of a reflective, submissive state toward one's self and others.

Does humility play a part in your life? If yes, how? If no, why not?

_____

_____

_____

_____

_____

How can humility become a strength in your life?

_____

_____

_____

_____

_____

SHORTCOMINGS

The shortcomings being discussed here are the character defects you identified in Step Six. Though it sounds funny, it can be hard to let go of your shortcomings, as they may have become your personal defenses or areas of comfort. But know this: These shortcomings are keeping you from becoming the best person you can be in life! Asking them to be removed only means freedom and a more valued sense of well-being.

What will be the hardest part of asking your Higher Power to remove your shortcomings?

_____

_____

_____

_____

How will you deal with this?

_____

_____

_____

_____

How can you be sure you will not hold something back?

_____

_____

_____

_____

_____

Have you ever asked a Higher Power to remove your character defects? Explain.

_____

_____

_____

_____

_____

Create a new list of *all* your character defects that you are willing to have your Higher Power remove from you.

_____

_____

_____

_____

ART DIRECTIVE

7.1 Letting Go Drawing

Goals:

- To create an image of yourself letting go of something holding you back in your recovery.

- To identify what new goals you are reaching for in your recovery.

- To understand what needs to change for you to reach your goals.

Materials:

- Paper (larger paper preferred)

- Drawing supplies (markers, colored pencils, pencils, pens, etc.)

Directions:

Make two tracings of your hand on a larger sheet of paper (or two pieces of paper if needed). First, trace your hand in the upper left hand corner so that it is reaching up away from you. Next, flip the paper around and again trace your hand in the upper left hand corner so that it is reaching down toward you once you flip it back around. If using two pieces of paper, designate one for each hand. On the hand reaching up, away from you, decorate it depicting what it is you are reaching for (new goals in recovery). On the hand reaching down, toward you, decorate it depicting what it is you're willing to let go of in recovery (personal weakness, addiction, etc.).

Example:

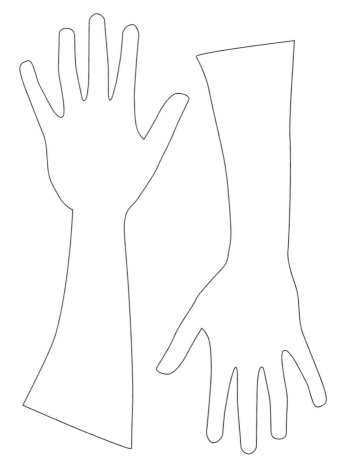

LETTING GO DRAWING: WRITTEN REFLECTIONS

What was this experience like for you?

_____

_____

_____

What are you willing to let go of? What are you reaching for?

_____

_____

_____

_____

_____

What is the hardest part of letting something go? Explain.

_____

_____

_____

_____

What is the hardest part of reaching for something? Explain.

_____

_____

_____

_____

What did you learn about yourself by doing this activity?

_____

_____

_____

_____

_____

Create your own personal prayer/personal admission, asking your Higher Power to remove these character defects.

_____

_____

_____

_____

List qualities you would like your Higher Power to give to you.

_____

_____

_____

_____

Why are these qualities important to you?

_____

_____

_____

_____

What changes have you noticed in yourself as a result of working Step Seven?

_____

_____

_____

_____

How is this step essential to your recovery?

_____

_____

_____

_____

ART DIRECTIVE

7.2 A Personal Gift

Goals:
- To recognize the hard work you have completed thus far in your recovery journey.
- To imagine what the removal of your shortcomings may bring to you.
- To promote positive and healthy self-care and gratitude.

Materials:
- Paper
- Drawing supplies (markers, colored pencils, pencils, pens, etc.)

Directions:

On your paper, create an outline of a gift box as best you can. There is an example below for guidance. In the box, draw something you wish to reward yourself with for the hard work you have endured thus far in your recovery. Remember to decorate the box and wrapping.

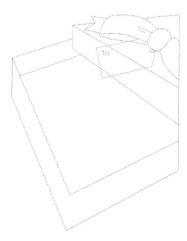

A PERSONAL GIFT: WRITTEN REFLECTIONS

What was this experience like for you?

_____

_____

_____

What gift did you decide to give to yourself?

_____

_____

_____

_____

How and why did you choose this gift? Of what importance is it to you?

_____

_____

_____

_____

_____

What other gifts would you like to give yourself?

_____

_____

_____

_____

Do you feel you are worthy of giving yourself a gift? If yes, explain. If no, how can you help yourself feel worthy of receiving a personal gift?

_____

_____

_____

_____

_____

What did you learn about yourself by doing this activity?

_____

_____

_____

_____

Asking for your shortcomings to be removed does not necessarily mean you are 100 percent free from them. We often let things go that are destructive in our lives yet are quick to reach back for them. Do not be discouraged if you see one pop back up. Simply repeat the personal prayer/admission you created earlier in this chapter as needed. You no longer have to be burdened with the negative feelings or resentments from your past. Now is the time to move forward with responsible, positive thinking.

STEP EIGHT

We made a list of all persons we had harmed and became willing to make amends to them all.

QUESTIONS

Define the following terms in your own words:

List

_____

_____

Harmed

_____

_____

Willing

_____

_____

Amends

_____

_____

What does this step mean to you?

_____

_____

_____

_____

Write this step in your own words.

_____

_____

_____

What is the difference between making an amend and an apology?

_____

_____

_____

_____

LIST OF AMENDS

Making amends with someone does not mean only saying "I'm sorry." Making amends goes further in requiring you to come to terms with your past actions toward people, understanding how your actions affected them personally, and letting them know how you recognize the pain you may have caused them. Saying you're sorry is important, but make sure you are not just saying empty words.

In the spaces provided, list every person you need to make amends with, why you need to make these amends, and how you are going to do this. There is an additional checklist next to every name in order for you to keep track of your progress.

Hint: Don't forget to add yourself!

Example:

X	Person to whom Amends will be Made	Why Amends Need to be Made	How the Amends will be Made
	Brother	I stole money from his wallet to buy alcohol.	I will go over to his house and make my amends with him face to face.
	Friend	I snitched on him and he went to prison.	I will not be able to visit him, therefore, I will make my amends to him through a letter.

Your List of Amends:

X	Person to whom Amends will be Made	Why Amends Need to be Made	How the Amends will be Made

How can your Higher Power help prepare you to make amends to others?

_____

_____

_____

_____

_____

How are you going to prepare yourself for making these amends?

_____

_____

_____

_____

What changes will you see in your life after you forgive yourself?

_____

_____

_____

_____

What is the hardest part of forgiving yourself?

_____

_____

_____

_____

_____

How is this step essential to your recovery?

_____

_____

_____

_____

ART DIRECTIVE

8.1 Road Drawing

Goals:
- To reflect upon your personal journey and to possibly see what role relationships have played throughout your life.
- To identify possible roadblocks that you have encountered along your journey of recovery.
- To recognize you are traveling the path you have chosen for yourself.

Materials:
- Paper
- Drawing supplies (markers, colored pencils, pencils, pens, etc.)

Directions:
On your paper, draw a road. Feel free to depict the road(s) anyway you wish, adding signs, intersections, people, and/or places.

ROAD DRAWING: WRITTEN REFLECTIONS

What was this experience like for you?

_____

_____

_____

Describe your road.

_____

_____

_____

_____

Does the road tell a story?

_____

_____

_____

_____

What is happening along the road?

_____

_____

_____

_____

_____

How do you feel about your road?

_____

_____

_____

_____

What did you learn about yourself by doing this activity?

_____

_____

_____

_____

_____

_____

_____

_____

ART DIRECTIVE

8.2 Cave Drawing

Goals:
- To develop an understanding of the items you value most in life, including personal relationships and/or material possessions.
- To clarify what items bring you the most peace and serenity.
- To identify which of these items are missing from your life.

Materials:
- Paper
- Drawing supplies (markers, colored pencils, pencils, pens, etc.)

Directions:
Draw a cave. In it, place everything you would want with you to sustain yourself for an undetermined length of time.

CAVE DRAWING: WRITTEN REFLECTIONS

What was this experience like for you?

_____

_____

_____

Describe your cave.

_____

_____

_____

_____

_____

What did you place with you in the cave?

_____

_____

_____

_____

_____

Are these things you have in your life presently? If no, explain how you could obtain these items.

_____

_____

_____

_____

_____

What did you learn about yourself by doing this activity?

_____

_____

_____

_____

_____

Hopefully you have made a thorough list of people with whom you need to make amends. I hope you understand how important it is to take responsibility for your past actions in this way. Instead of feeling nervous or scared to make these amends, be grateful for the opportunity to attempt to make things right with others in your life.

.

STEP NINE

We made direct amends to such people wherever possible, except when to do so would injure them or others.

QUESTIONS

Define the following terms in your own words:

Direct amends

_____

_____

Wherever possible

_____

_____

Injure

_____

_____

Others

_____

_____

What does this step mean to you?

_____

_____

_____

_____

Write this step in your own words.

_____

_____

_____

How have the previous eight steps prepared you for making amends?

_____

_____

_____

_____

Why is taking this step essential to your recovery?

_____

_____

_____

_____

_____

_____

_____

ART DIRECTIVE

9.1 Forgiveness Drawing

Goals:
- To define what forgiveness means to you.
- To think of the different ways forgiveness can take shape.
- To recognize the power of personal forgiveness and its importance in the recovery journey.

Materials:
- Paper
- Drawing supplies (markers, colored pencils, pencils, pens, etc.)

Directions:
Reflect on the word *forgiveness* and the meaning it has in your life. Draw an image of this idea of forgiveness.

FORGIVENESS DRAWING: WRITTEN REFLECTIONS

What was this experience like for you?

_____

_____

_____

How does forgiveness play a role in your life?

_____

_____

_____

Does forgiveness come easy to you? Why or why not?

_____

_____

_____

_____

Describe your drawing.

_____

_____

_____

_____

_____

How does it feel to look at your image of forgiveness?

_____

_____

_____

_____

What did you learn about yourself by doing this activity?

_____

_____

_____

_____

APOLOGIES AND AMENDS

What is the importance of you making amends?

_____

_____

_____

_____

_____

What do you feel is most important? Explain.

_____

_____

_____

_____

_____

What are you most afraid of in taking this step?

_____

_____

_____

_____

How can these fears be overcome?

_____

_____

_____

_____

_____

How can your Higher Power help you through this step?

_____

_____

_____

_____

How do you expect to feel after making these amends?

_____

_____

_____

How can you make amends where direct contact is not possible?

_____

_____

_____

_____

_____

Can meditation, prayer, or journaling help with this? Why or why not?

_____

_____

_____

_____

_____

Before moving forward, take time to complete all the amends you have written out from Step Eight. It is preferred to make all amends face to face; however, you may not always have that option. A phone call, a letter in the mail, or even an e-mail may work better in such situations. No matter what route you choose to take, remember to be humble and sincere with every amend.

How do you feel after the amends have been made?

_____

_____

_____

_____

Can you describe the difference in your life now as opposed to before making amends?

_____

_____

_____

_____

_____

How is this step essential to your recovery?

_____

_____

_____

_____

_____

Abandon yourself to God as you understand God. Admit your faults to Him and to your fellows. Clear away the wreckage of your past.

Alcoholics Anonymous, 2001, p. 164

ART DIRECTIVE

9.2 Past, Present, Future Drawings

Goals:
- To recognize where you came from and why you entered recovery.
- To increase awareness of who you are today in relation to the past and the future.
- To gain perspective on your life journey.

Materials:
- Paper
- Drawing supplies (markers, colored pencils, pencils, pens, etc.)

Directions:
For this exercise you will be creating three different drawings. First, create a drawing of yourself prior to entering recovery. Second, create a drawing of yourself as you are right now in your recovery journey. Lastly, create a drawing of where you see yourself in the near future (you can choose in the next several months, year, etc.).

PAST, PRESENT, FUTURE DRAWINGS: WRITTEN REFLECTIONS

What was this experience like for you?

_____

_____

_____

Describe all three of your drawings.

_____

_____

_____

_____

_____

_____

_____

Which one is most significant to you? Why?

_____

_____

_____

_____

Describe your future drawing. Is this an image that could become a reality? Why or why not?

_____

_____

_____

_____

What did you learn about yourself by doing this activity?

_____

_____

_____

_____

Talk about true humbleness. Saying you're sorry and admitting to others your past wrongs is hard. But hopefully by this point you have done all you can do. Remember mistakes will still happen. You are human after all! Just remember to be patient with yourself and content with what you are able to accomplish. Believe it or not, making amends with others does get easier the more you do it.

STEP TEN

We continued to take a personal inventory and when we were wrong promptly admitted it.

QUESTIONS

Define the following terms in your own words:

Continued

_____

_____

Personal inventory

_____

_____

Wrong

_____

_____

Promptly admitted

_____

_____

What does this step mean to you?

_____

_____

_____

Write this step in your own words.

_____

_____

How is continued maintenance of the previous steps critical to your recovery?

_____

_____

_____

_____

What is one nonconstructive behavior you see reappearing in your daily life? How will you deal with this?

_____

_____

_____

_____

How do you plan to continually take a personal inventory in your life?

_____

_____

_____

_____

Will you take an inventory on a daily or weekly basis? Which do you think would be more beneficial to you?

_____

_____

_____

_____

What benefits do you see in taking a daily inventory of your life?

_____

_____

_____

_____

How will a daily inventory help you evaluate your behaviors?

_____

_____

_____

_____

How will a daily inventory improve your relationships with others?

_____

_____

_____

_____

How can promptly admitting your faults ease your relations with others?

_____

_____

_____

_____

What would happen if you didn't resolve angry and negative feelings as they arose?

_____

_____

_____

_____

Describe the changes you see in your life as a result of taking these steps.

_____

_____

_____

_____

How is this step essential to your recovery?

_____

_____

_____

_____

_____

ART DIRECTIVE

10.1 Self-Care Collage

Goals:

- To increase your desire to indulge in personal activities vital to your recovery.
- To brainstorm different activities you enjoy and would connect with personally.
- To enable yourself to engage in positive activities for your emotional and physical growth.

Materials:

- Paper (larger paper preferred)
- Collage materials, scissors, glue
- Drawing supplies (markers, colored pencils, pencils, pens, etc.)

Directions:
Think of different things you enjoy doing for yourself. Do you enjoy going for walks, taking a bath, playing with your children, or listening to music? Create a collage from images that represent different activities you would be willing to engage in for relaxation, physical growth, and emotional stability.

(If collage materials are not available to you, sketch out related images using drawing supplies.)

SELF-CARE COLLAGE: WRITTEN REFLECTIONS

What was this experience like for you?

_____

_____

_____

What images were included in your collage?

_____

_____

_____

_____

Which of these items do you already do? Which would you like to start doing?

_____

_____

_____

_____

How does it feel to see the different activities you could engage in for personal growth?

_____

_____

_____

_____

_____

What did you learn about yourself by doing this activity?

_____

_____

_____

_____

_____

Art Directive

10.2 Personal Crest

Goals:
- To develop an awareness of who you are as an individual.
- To understand how your characteristics and strengths can help you in your recovery.
- To clarify ways you can strengthen your defenses in relapse situations.

Materials:
- Paper
- Drawing supplies (markers, colored pencils, pencils, pens, etc.)

Directions:
Create an outline of a shield as shown in the example on the following page. Inside the shield, create symbols that give you strength in times of weakness. Use any or all of the following suggestions:
- Strength you learned/acquired from family/friends/a role model.
- Something you are good at (activity, skill, or hobby).
- Strength or symbol of your cultural heritage.
- A positive personal characteristic (reliable friend, good sense of humor, etc.).
- A personal motto or decorative writing of your name.

Example:

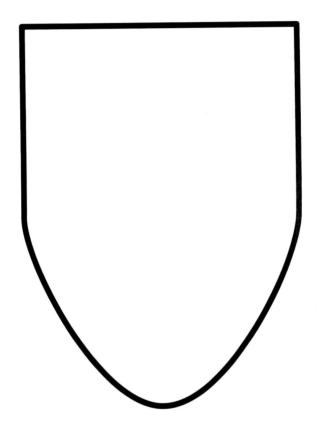

PERSONAL CREST: WRITTEN REFLECTIONS

What was this experience like for you?

_____

_____

_____

Describe the images on your crest.

_____

_____

_____

_____

_____

How will these images help "shield" you from relapse situations?

_____

_____

_____

_____

How does it feel to view all your personal strengths?

_____

_____

_____

_____

What title would you give this image?

_____

_____

What did you learn about yourself by doing this activity?

_____

_____

_____

_____

_____

Taking responsibility for your actions and making amends is an ongoing task. We are not perfect, nor will we ever be. And that's okay! Living a life in recovery means you will be constantly trying to better yourself and grow from daily experiences. Think back on any difficulties you encountered in completing Steps Four through Nine. Taking a daily or regular moral inventory of your actions ensures that your list of amends will never be that long again. But in order for that to happen, continually stay aware of your actions and your relationships with others.

STEP ELEVEN

We sought through prayer and meditation to improve our conscious contact with our Higher Power, praying only for knowledge of his will for us and the power to carry that out.

QUESTIONS

Define the following terms in your own words:

Prayer

_____

_____

Meditation

_____

_____

Conscious contact

_____

_____

Knowledge of his will

_____

_____

Power

_____

_____

What does this step mean to you?

_____

_____

_____

_____

Write this step in your own words.

_____

_____

_____

Having a relationship with your higher power is common to other personal relationships. It must be nurtured and cared for in order to grow. The following questions help guide you in finding a comfortable way to keep in contact with your Higher Power.

Where and how will you seek contact with your Higher Power?

_____

_____

_____

_____

_____

How often will you seek contact with your Higher Power?

_____

_____

_____

In what form will you seek contact? Prayer? Meditation? Journaling?

_____

_____

_____

What dialogue will you have with your Higher Power?

_____

_____

_____

_____

_____

How does it feel when you are in contact with your Higher Power?

_____

_____

_____

_____

_____

What will you discuss, disclose, or request from your Higher Power?

_____

_____

_____

_____

_____

_____

What difficulties, if any, do you have in developing a conscious contact with your Higher Power?

_____

_____

_____

What do you believe causes these difficulties?

_____

_____

_____

_____

How will you deal with these difficulties?

_____

_____

_____

_____

_____

Do you ever have doubts when communicating with your Higher Power? Explain.

_____

_____

_____

_____

_____

_____

Where do these doubts come from?

_____

_____

_____

_____

How can they be dealt with?

_____

_____

_____

_____

_____

In the spaces provided, develop your own personal daily prayer that is meaningful to you in your life.

_____

_____

_____

_____

_____

What benefits have you seen as a result of working this step?

_____

_____

_____

_____

How is this step essential to your recovery?

_____

_____

_____

_____

Faith alone is insufficient. To be vital, faith must be accompanied by self sacrifice and unselfish, constructive action.

Alcoholics Anonymous, 2001, p. 93

ART DIRECTIVE

11.1 Safe Place Drawing

Goals:
- To envision a place where you feel safe and secure from your addiction.
- To create a visual representation of your safe place.
- To reflect on items and feelings that make you feel safe, secure, happy, and content.

Materials:
- Paper
- Drawing supplies (markers, colored pencils, pencils, pens, etc.)

Directions:
Think of a place where you have no fears, no worries, and no doubts. Draw this place.

SAFE PLACE DRAWING: WRITTEN REFLECTIONS

What was this experience like for you?

_____

_____

_____

_____

Describe your drawing.

_____

_____

_____

_____

_____

What does your safe place look like? Who is present? What items are there?

_____

_____

_____

_____

_____

_____

Was it difficult envisioning a comfortable and safe place? Explain.

_____

_____

_____

_____

What title would you give this drawing?

_____

_____

_____

_____

What did you learn about yourself by doing this activity?

_____

_____

_____

_____

_____

You are not alone! And you do not have to go through this journey alone. Continue to use the personal prayer or admission of surrender you created in Step Three on a regular basis. Humble yourself regularly and do not be afraid to ask for help or spiritual direction from your Higher Power when needed.

STEP TWELVE

Having had a spiritual awakening as a result of these steps, we tried to carry this message to others and to practice these principles in all our affairs.

QUESTIONS

Define the following terms in your own words:

Spiritual awakening

_____

_____

Carry the message

_____

_____

Practice these principles

_____

_____

All our affairs

_____

_____

What does this step mean to you?

_____

_____

Write this step in your own words.

_____

_____

_____

How have other people in recovery helped you through your own recovery? Explain.

_____

_____

_____

_____

_____

_____

How did it feel being helped through a tough time in your life?

_____

_____

_____

_____

_____

What ways do you reach out to others right now?

_____

_____

_____

_____

_____

_____

How will you reach out in the future?

_____

_____

_____

_____

_____

_____

How have you helped another person in recovery in the past few weeks?

_____

_____

_____

_____

_____

_____

What qualities do you feel a sponsor should possess? Explain.

_____

_____

_____

_____

_____

_____

Have you thought about becoming a sponsor?

_____

_____

What qualities do you feel you have that would benefit someone else in his or her recovery?

_____

_____

_____

_____

How could you "practice these principles in all [your] affairs?"

_____

_____

_____

_____

Do you feel this step can ever be completed? Why or why not?

_____

_____

_____

_____

How are you going to put this step into practice in your own life?

_____

_____

_____

_____

_____

_____

How is this step essential to your recovery?

_____

_____

_____

_____

_____

Showing others who suffer how we were given help is the very thing which makes life seem so worth while to us now. Cling to the thought that, in God's hands, the dark past is the greatest possession you have—the key to life and happiness for others. With it you can avert death and misery for them.

Alcoholics Anonymous, 2001, p. 124

ART DIRECTIVE

12.1 Recovery Trading Cards

Goals:
- To explore reinforcing statements that are encouragements in the recovery process.
- To create pocket-sized reminders of positive reflections.
- To share with other people in recovery optimistic thoughts you have learned in your recovery process.

Materials:
- Index cards
- Drawing supplies (markers, colored pencils, pencils, pens, etc.)

Directions:
Illustrate each card with a positive slogan from twelve-step meetings, words of encouragement in treatment, and/or with affirmative, optimistic images. Keep these cards in designated places around your home or office or pass them out to other people in recovery or who are special in your life.

RECOVERY TRADING CARDS: WRITTEN REFLECTIONS

What was this experience like for you?

_____

_____

_____

_____

Describe the cards you created.

_____

_____

_____

_____

_____

_____

How can these affirming words or illustrations be applied to your own life?

_____

_____

_____

_____

How can you share these with other people?

_____

_____

_____

_____

How can you keep them with you?

_____

_____

_____

_____

What did you learn about yourself by doing this activity?

_____

_____

_____

_____

ART DIRECTIVE

12.2 Drawings of Gratitude

Goals:

- To express your feelings of gratitude thus far in your journey.
- To remind yourself of the good things that have been given to you.
- To recognize there is more in life than yourself.

Materials:

- Paper
- Drawing supplies (markers, colored pencils, pencils, pens, etc.)

Directions:

Draw your current feeling of gratitude and what you are grateful for at this moment. You are encouraged to create these gratitude drawings on a regular basis.

DRAWINGS OF GRATITUDE: WRITTEN REFLECTIONS

What was this experience like for you?

_____

_____

_____

_____

What does your current feeling of gratitude look like?

_____

_____

_____

_____

What are some other items you are grateful for in your life?

_____

_____

_____

_____

Has it been a long time since you have felt grateful? If yes, explain what it feels like now. If no, why not?

_____

_____

_____

_____

_____

_____

What did you learn about yourself by doing this activity?

_____

_____

_____

_____

You have been given a very special gift. What a great way to show your gratitude for your blessings by sharing your experiences with others going through similar struggles. You are able to show others hope by the way you live your life, the decisions you make, and your relationships with others. There is no promise that life magically becomes perfect upon entering recovery, but it does become more manageable and more enjoyable.

It is my hope that you have grown from this experience and made new realizations about your life and your purpose. Never be afraid to return to any of these art directives or questions for continued support. Keep in mind, the more energy you put into bettering yourself, the better the result! And remember to laugh often, care for others continually, and love yourself always. You are worth it!

YOUR NOTES

_____

_____

_____

_____

_____

_____

_____

_____

_____

_____

_____

_____

_____

_____

_____

_____

_____

PERSONAL PHONE NUMBERS

Name   *Number*

_____ _____

_____ _____

_____ _____

_____ _____

_____ _____

_____ _____

_____ _____

_____ _____

_____ _____

_____ _____

_____ _____

_____ _____

_____ _____

_____ _____

Alcoholics Anonymous Official Web site
www.alcoholics-anonymous.org

AA World Services Inc.
(212) 870–3400

National Institute on Drug Abuse
http://www.nida.nih.gov

National Institute on Alcohol Abuse and Alcoholism
http://www.niaaa.nih.gov/NewsEvents/NewsReleases/match.htm

Faces and Voices of Recovery
http://www.facesandvoicesofrecovery.org/about/faq.php

Substance Abuse & Mental Health Services Administration
http://www.samhsa.gov

RECOMMENDED READINGS

Alcoholics Anonymous
AA World Services Inc.
2001

Twelve Steps and Twelve Traditions
AA World Services Inc.
1981

Daily Reflections
AA World Services Inc.
1990

Living Sober
AA World Services Inc.
1998

Experience, Strength & Hope
AA World Services Inc.
2003

Understanding the Twelve Steps
Terrence T. Gorski
1989

Visual Journaling: Going Deeper Than Words
Barbara Ganim & Susan Fox
1999

The Picture of Health
Lucia Capacchione
1996

The Language of Letting Go
Melody Beattie
1990

ART DIRECTIVES: SOURCES

I have attempted to reference each of the art directives back to the proper source; however, understand that not all of them can be traced back to one person. Therefore, the references listed are the most original I was able to retrieve. Several of the art directives are not referenced, as they were either created by myself or had no background information available.

Step	Art Directive
Step 1	Collage of Chaos; Life Line[1]; Picture of Powerlessness[1]
Step 2	Image of Higher Power[1]; Bridge to Recovery[2]
Step 3	My Will[1]; Turning it Over Collage[2]; Circles of Strength
Step 4	Wall Drawing; Ugly Picture Drawing[1]; Secret Drawing
Step 5	Broken-Wall Drawing; Anger/Peace Collage
Step 6	Pictures of Personal Shortcomings; Five Years From Now Drawing
Step 7	Letting Go Drawing[3]; A Personal Gift[3]
Step 8	Road Drawing[4]; Cave Drawing
Step 9	Forgiveness Drawing; Past, Present, Future Drawings[3]
Step 10	Self Care Collage; Personal Crest[3]
Step 11	Safe Place
Step 12	Recovery Trading Cards; Drawings of Gratitude[3]

Reference: [1] C.A. Carroll, [2] Kell Julliard, [3] Libby Schmanke, [4] Michael Hanes

BIBLIOGRAPHY

Alcoholics Anonymous. (4th ed.). (2001). New York. Alcoholics Anonymous World Services, Inc.

Carroll, C. A. (1990). *Use of the Twelve Steps of Alcoholics Anonymous in Art Therapy Groups With Substance Abusers.* Unpublished master's thesis, College of Notre Dame, Belmont, CA.

Hanes, M. J. (1997). *Roads to the Unconscious: A Manual for Understanding Road Drawings.* Oklahoma City, OK: Wood 'N' Barnes Publishing.

Julliard, K. (1999). The twelve steps and art therapy [Monograph]. American Art Therapy Association, Inc., 1–24.

Schmanke, L. (2004). Sample directives for art therapy with substance abusers. Emporia State University.

Twelve Steps and Twelve Traditions. (1981). New York. Alcoholics Anonymous World Services, Inc.